[praise for Em J Parsley]

"Em J Parsley's *the anonym gospels* is an inwardly expansive chapbook of poems. Parsley's speaker comes to us tenderly from a landscape of haphazard violence: 'The body is not made / for thinness, nor is it made for preservation.' Reading this book is like walking toward a soft light in which we shed our own certainty with every step closer. 'I love / you now and I / would have loved you then.' Follow the poet Em J Parsley— his poems welcome and warm the dark of us."
– C.T. Salazar, author of *Headless John the Baptist Hitchhiking*

"'What we say when we want / a hand to hold is not unreasonable.' Em J Parsley has written a book I wish I could send back in time, 40 years ago to my evangelical Tennessee tomboy barely-hanging-on heart. It has been too long since I experienced this transcendence of language at its most honest, which is to say names that are exact in their namelessness: 'boy-girl-other, mudslush, empty air above the rows where the corn cobs used to breathe.' Like any good news that is true, *the anonym gospels* hold grief and beauty, connection and rupture, the earthly and the ethereal in one open hand. Here is a book that would save so many queer and trans youth (and adults) from the hell of aloneness that results from being told the divine can't live inside us. Reaching and full of grace, this should be required reading in the churches of open fields, all across the south."
– TC Tolbert, author of *Gephyromania* and *The Quiet Practices*

the anonym gospels

Em J Parsley

APRIL GLOAMING

Winner of the
Apogee Poetry Chapbook Award

Publisher's Cataloguing-in-Publication Data

Parsley, Em J
   The anonym gospels / written by Em J Parsley
   ISBN: 978-1-953932-23-5

1. Poetry: General 2. Poetry: American - General 3. Poetry: LGBTQ+
I. Title II. Author

Library of Congress Control Number: 2023950646

[contents]

anonym I

anonym II

[contents]

anonym III

anonym IV

an apocryphal gospel

To everyone who shared with me the good news.

[anonym I]

[when I discovered the word "all"]

I shaped it like a prayer: is that all
you see? Is that all you know?
all & all & all &

all like always &
all like almost &
all like alright &

all right &
in all my days—what
days?

Days haven't happened
since I saw my naked 13-
year-old body in the mirror

—all my bones—hips
jutting out
of control.

I read in *Seventeen* that
not all boys like tits
& I was relieved even

though I didn't
want boys—not all? No, not
any. Surely not

every body needs
to be claimed. Surely
this body doesn't

need me & surely
when you told me
you knew all of me

you didn't mean *this*
—you didn't mean *all*—
how could you, when

I, 13, all-wise &
full of alleluia,
did not?

Seventeen said
that if I broke my bones
again & again & always

my hips would recall a shape
they never knew & you would
say it's alright & I would be all right.

*[the same god who told me being gay was a sin when I was eight sold me t
on the down low ten years later]*

Tell me it was gentle,
        like when my mother brushed
              the hair from my forehead and said,
                if God wanted you to fly, He would have called
you Icarus

                    and with her feverish
     fingertips

                  running through my roots, I asked,
                    do you want to be
                    Daedalus?

[name added to "when I transition" list: Icarus]

—

I wanted to give you
a single, easy command, like so:
        Love your neighbor as yourself, except for that kid in third grade
            who called you a Dyke
                which you thought was a man's name so you
                    said, actually, my dad's name is Eddie.

It's not that I wanted you
to love me less, of course,

it's just that your lips were melted
      butter, dripping
            down my cheeks without ever reaching my mouth—

[name added: "Actually, It's Eddie"]

—

When you said
    golden   wounded   light
        I saw the puddle of blood in the back
        corner of the wheelbarrow, shifting,
        gathering ice, moving to rigor
        mortis before her body could catch up.

[name added: frost-bitten. 7 am. sunrise.]

—

            I don't know why I
            expected
            you to know my name
            when you
            had never seen the
                    orderly, headless
            bodies of harvested corn
                stalks like
            terracotta soldiers protecting
            the bones of deer and

I don't know why I
couldn't hold a knife
the way that's needed
        in order to gut
a doe proper, or why my
cloudy breath moved
constant in front of my
mouth, insisted I was
        still alive, why
I could kiss everything
but your lips, crystalized—

[name added: empty air above the rows where the corn cobs used to
        breathe]
[name added: red stain of cardinal against brown december landscape as
        my fingers turn purple]

[name added: Abel. Hebrew.
meaning   breath
meaning   son
meaning   I flew until the fever caught fire in every one of my bones,
        and then I fell]

[three bodies and the memory of a fourth while the earth turns slowly]

And when you pivot, as a creaking garden gate
in late fall, know that you'll have to swing
back and remember—but not yet. See first:
       the silver rifle caressed
       in dewy grass;
       your nails encrusted
       with deer's blood; gnaw
       at your fingers and taste
       —iron: biting at the golden teddy bear charm, expelling his
         stale air—
       a still-dying doe as she shifts
       into something useful for you. Turn

on that weight and look—no, not at that. Look:
       the bloated calf's corpse you pulled
       through a snowy field loosened
       your fingers' numb grip on
       the back hooves, slipped
       on mudslush, wind kicked
       from your lungs, you were
       —closing your eyes, throat, fist around the charm's ruby
         heart—
       breathless for a week. Remember

when you face it—no, not just yet. Remember:
    the cornsnake, tortured by the neighborhood
    boys, wrapped in tape and spray painted
    gold, how you sat with her for hours,
    soaking her bound body in soapy water until the tape
    sloughed from the scales and she
    could breathe again, and you
    —would steal his lungs if you could—
    —would shove the charm down his throat—
    —would see how he likes the helpless cry of choking silence
coming from his own lips—
    fed her mice even though you love
    mice because she is gentle in her consumption.

Now here's the carefully calculated weight

of turning on your heel
to look it in the eye as it asks
you to live—yes, live—
    the stiff knuckles working
    through your tomboy rat's nest hair and
    his clinging breath on your ear that pushes
    across your jaw, past your cheek, seeps
    into your body, the only one you have, through
    the eardrums and nostrils and teeth and the little golden
    bear with the ruby for a heart, imprinted
    in your palm by the pressure from your thumb—
    this is full and leaking what is his. You are too young
    to understand that his hands shouldn't move
    like that and you shouldn't breathe like that. You did not

know until you laid next to a sleeping woman for the first
time that breath is supposed to be an equal give
and take and not a series of syncopated
seizures where your lungs try to escape with
the memory that they were once wings. Step

just inches away from that face and remember
his hands because you must, but
also remember your palm on the dying doe,

which was mercy. Do not forget mercy,
and do not forget the spot where your heel twisted
into the dirt as you turned, where your lungs
re-learned the steady and even affair
of a resting breath, where you crushed
the little bear, wrenched the ruby from its core, set
it on your tongue, and felt its weight throughout.

[anonym II]

[death of the hen in three syllables]

You foresaw her death alone, right
where you left her. If you had allowed her
the comfort of other bodies, her brood-mates
would've pecked at her corpse, and you
would wake to this purview:
that the white hen with black flecks like
pepper ate her eyes. Your love is
too cracked to understand the treachery
of animals more generous than you.

Gather her unopened body
in the plastic Kroger bag like she's
a piece of dog shit, knot the ties twice, begin
the march to beyond the apple orchard,
her shriveled spider-corpse-talons
straining to rise to the canopy
above, her domed skull ushered
to land, as if it already knew
where bones go.

When I was a child,
I hung from the sofa, hair brushing
the floor, shoes pressed to the ceiling
as my mother held one-person
spelling bees, and I reigned supreme.
Eight years old, so proud of "endurance."
2 e's and 2 n's, that broken pipe "c," and where
did they go? I knew.

You chose her name from a picture
book of your bedtime routine, a name you won't
speak now. She took it with her.
Say it fast—endurance.
Now: en-dur-ance.
Hear that *ah* right before your
teeth and tongue meet
to make that "c" hiss? That's
where your name sits—in the ah
of deconstructed endurance.

I was granted a name and it is
mine and I'll never
lose it, even after
its death. I killed it,
trowled my hands into the doughy,
rain-stricken earth, pushing aside
bundled moss and joyous earthworms
not six feet under, perhaps two,
maybe three.

How many sounds
are in e-lec-tric, little Emily?
Em-i-ly. The corpse in the Kroger bag
and your head collide when you swing
upside-down and tell your mother
how to spell em-u-late—mother who
missed home so much she packed you tight
like a set of china and carried you back
to robin-brown and summer corn. What about
tuh-bac-cuh, little Ducky?
how many sounds?
count them with claps. One-two-
three, lose-your-
breath from the vertigo
of the plastic bag swaying
past your thigh as you walk the edge
of the cornfield
and say it,
en-
dur-
ance.
Consider the

breaths, tally the
sounds.

I can't touch
the dead hen with
bare hands, lest the mites
quitting the cooling body

own their new home
in me, and then who
will pull me away—alone,
to keep the pepper hen from
pecking out my eyes; and who
will lose my name for me; who
will cradle me in the plastic Kroger bag,
spine running down their open
palms where their right and left pinkies
meet, fingers curled up
and around my skull, reaching
toward a cracked love while the
weight of my hair
slips through their knuckles.

[theodicy]

Only the sadist loves being strung
across the ocean, organs beaded

on a silver cord—heart,
liver, pancreas curing

in the open salted air, wounds
a'gaping. The body is not made

for thinness, nor is it made for preservation.
Strained coast to coast, a tendon should

snap, and if it does not, it hurts
and hurts. Do stop me if you think this is silly,

but bodies are made for trembling and being
held in their trembling—they are not a horizon,

and nothing, neither Chance nor God,
would create life only to watch

it sunset itself with salt-choked wailing.
The briny heart still beats, even suspended

breaths above the choppy waves.
What we say when we want
a hand to hold is not unreasonable.

[portrait of creature-feeling]

Here is the premise:
> —do you mind? sometimes straightforward
> is the *way to go,* no harm in that—

I am slight but scrappy, you are
> strong but tired.
This doesn't mean I'll win, because
exhaustion is funny and fluctuating and it's silly but
sometimes there is the urge to wish
it were all already over
> —the whole of it: society, earth, living,
you—me,
> and everything else—

still, we are standing. thoughtless little
zombies—sprouts, rootless—but standing
> still.
Other times:
> my body collapses.

Premise:
> when you were a boy, people called
> > you beautiful:
> > > a perfect and genderless
> > childhood trait
> *—sweet beautiful boy—*

then you grew
        up and lost this modifier on the side
of the road, picked up handsome and good-
        looking, and you don't complain, but they're not

the same. Premise:
        we swerve to avoid hitting
a deer. They say
you should not. Slow yourself, yes, but hit it dead-
on, the way galaxies collide:
        flesh against flesh—metal amidst fur—
        bone into gravel.

Premise: any more pressure
        to the thing that is
        my body, it—I—they—we—the whole of it—will shatter.

Mid-point:
        we fight. It is
violent. The crowd is violent.
                The whole of it: violent and sweet. sweet like a zom
                bie. sweet like a boy.

Conclusion: neither of us
        win. Our debris-like limbs splinter
        and reform.
The beautiful boy in the audience hails our transformation.

[anonym III]

[eschaton]

The rapture begins in your wrists—therapist,
after you tell her your parents will never love you

the way you want them to: "where do you feel
that sorrow in your body?"

Text from dad: "the end is high."
Ha, what a typo. Your adrenaline spikes regardless—

trembling hands and a head that's forgotten the fear
of God but limbs remember the kneeling,

forehead in hands,
forehead to carpet,

to dirt,
to train track.

"In my shoulders," you tell her, hunched forward
in your chair, the permanent slump of one who

has not prayed in years but knows the line
the spine creates, rounded at the skull

like the shepherd's staff. On the day the world ends,
you fulfill this prophecy: gnashing of teeth—a semi-circular, contemplative

grinding. Half-eaten toast, limp with butter. Twisting
pen in hand, stir the air, stare out the kitchen window—

across the country, your dad prays for his own toast,
this morning, your soul. We—no, you and he—
begin like this, always.

[hymns: untitled]

I.

in spite of all wants / I am not a healer / I am not / penitent enough for
the gods nor / resolute enough for the unbeliever / my childhood dog
shakes, dying, while I do my best to patch his disparate / parts together:
/ I hold him against / my chest & cover his eyes with a blanket & hum
/ hoping / his deaf body feels the reverberations / but / he must still
always die / & my chest, shifting / unbalanced

II.

& altogether wrong / will remain that way / not that it matters. not /
while tenderness is precise & / exacting yet never / surgical, & not while
I can swallow / my gasps & breathe / through my skin. not / while pose-
idon, who puppets each / of my inhales crafts shallow / pools / of mucus
in my lungs / & laughs at our / synchronized / anxious / wheezing / is
this too much?

III.

are my bones too hollow to be / of mammalian use? / if I remove my
favorite / knuckle could you boil / a single-serving broth / drink it
at midnight in your bare / numb feet / & learn the syllables trapped
beneath my breasts? / would you share / that with me?

IV.

the removal of an unwanted mass is not destruction / but maintenance
/ & I do not need to reconcile / the part of me that begs / to heal / with
the immutable / desire to terraform / the landscape of my body

Em J Parsley

[monologue regarding appalachia, voiced to an empty room]

Picture me: I bring the half-crushed deer skull up
to eye level, some boy-girl-other hamlet. It is late
spring and I am in love with the sound of the dead
corn stalks crunching under my boots—it is good:
a ripe sound that heralds the coming of vivid
newness and when I inspect bones

there are rules, questions to ask. First, the teeth:
are they sunk into the soft earth where the jaw
                lies to rest?
Second, are the eye sockets gnawed by coyotes,
                whose scavenging ways I respect?
Third, what will I do with the life I can't
                take back?

My skin breaks out in rashes whenever the weather shifts—
how my body pushes back against change, how
the past looks, snow, alighting on grass too warm
                to hold its shape—
my face, my chest, stagnant while the seasons snap
in and out of place. Picture me:

girl-prince of Appalachia with a plan of action.
First off, I make ophelia my constant companion
and lover in the loving sense of the word.
Second, I take her to the best view Kentucky's got.
We watch the sun sink low while we sink even lower,
and when the moon rises, we trade clothes
and walk to the nearby village and they call her
"sweet boy" and me "pretty girl," and they weave
                dogwood in our hair
and when the clock strikes twelve, I transform
back into pretty boy, her, sweet girl.

Third, just before the night sky goes pale, bluegrass
                and daffodils
beneath our moon-shining toes, we see specters
in the snow, falling, never settling—wait, hear now.

My father is not dead, only the ghost of some undefined
manliness passed on to me and my sisters to make
us dual out our shotgun revenge, but I am too transient, and they
are too sturdy, and the friction dissipates in inaction—
                accidental rebellion.

Picture me: I peer into the empty eye socket, expecting hollowness
and instead I am greeted by a wasp who has built its nest
in the half-dome, its legs tapping across the cranial suture,
looking for a fault line, something that might shift the stability
of what it has created. I don't like wasps, but I'm trying to, so
I put the skull down and don't pick it up again. It's better
for me and this skull to part ways. I haven't even prepared a soliloquy.

[anonym IV]

[the most efficient way to peel an orange]

I watch you peel an orange in the warm
summer evening, cross-legged,
concentrating rubix-cube style,
three parts stoicist, one part glee,

and one extra part that's not supposed to be
there, tucked in the way you tumble
over lyrics to an old Irish folk song.

Your futile efforts to remember
song lyrics are in my top ten
favorite things about you, placed at number
eight, used to be seven, recently usurped by me
catching you googling *what
is the most efficient way to peel an orange*

I don't think I'm supposed to know
this, and I don't know how I do, but
when you were eight, a pebble got
wedged in your roller skate—knee scraped

raw and a bruise so bad
the skin shifted to the rare
greenish-blue that categorizes
real nasty bruises. Your grim little mind
leapt to gangrene—too many books
on the American Civil War, which couldn't be
helped, being raised by that old man. It kills
me, how you accepted your battle-bleak
fate with gritted baby teeth, loosening
how mountains crumble—

how small you were. How brave.
how surprised you were
when the gangrene faded
and you didn't die. Fuck,
it makes me sad. You're here, with
your spiraling piles of spongy rind,
kissing my cheek, kissing
more than my cheek. I love
you now and I
would have loved you then.

[today, I give]

and I make
southern biscuits
rolling
and packing and
pressing
and cutting into
hearts for my ma,
wondering in what
ways I will not be
enough. fried eggs
from the coop and
the strawberry tops
I'll not discard;
they go
to the brood
in exchange for their hard
and natural work. just
because the eggs
appear every day
does not mean we
should take without
giving.

A friend
tells me there are
too many chickens
in my poems but
I need to explain
this over and over
until I am able
to understand
why I name
those who do not
care what I call
them. then again,
they also have no
wish that I would
disregard my ceremony
as long as they receive
strawberry tops and
scrap dough.

I can smell the butter
and flour
underneath
my fingernails and
when I give
them their titles,
this is duchess
and this is alaska
and this is georgie
and gin
and juke
it's simply because I want

something to mull
the syllables on:
consider clothes
on the mannequin
and names
on the animal and
chirping to hens
in their graceless
tongue, which is
sensible and
sweet and
requires no harm
from me.

[phone conversation with dad]
  monday, october 19, 2020

120V
I tell him, sometimes the bedroom lights go out if
the garage lights are on while the washer is going.
I toss out 208V and 240V and
        not 120V, that'll never
work, I say. the breaker. can the breaker
        handle it?

he rambles about amperage and I think about Bran-
don Teena and Gwen Araujo and how
martyrs have no armor but their own holy flesh
and I think about how there's no glory in seeing

them bleed. Clarification: garage
break-er, not house.

V O L T A G E, I ask. and write it like I'm just learn-
ing how to spell. care-ful, intentional space between the letters:

        v o l t a g e.
        v o l t a g e.

            v o l t a g e.

V O L T A G E: Scout Schultz, Kashmire Redd.
I pray to Lou Sullivan.

This is where the breaker system falls
apart: I hate the dark. I'm a bad dy-ke.
I have a terrible fear of eulogies.

208V
I never learned how to yell so their names
cy-cle through my head on repeat. 36 (U.S. and P.R., known)
dead this year.

what about a generat
-or? I ask my dad. Could I
hook it up to a generator? He starts
off again. I write. Hurried. Loop-
ing.

VOLTAGE. voltage.
voltage   voltage   volt-age   volt-age   volt-age
    v-o-l-t-a-g-e   oltage   voltAGE VOLTAGE   V O L T A G E

Dustin Parker
Neulisa Luciano Ruiz
Yampi Méndez Arocho
Monika Diamond
Lexi
Johanna Metzger
Serena Angelique Velázquez Ramos
Layla Pelaez Sánchez
Penélope Díaz Ramírez
Nina Pop
Helle Jae O'Regan

Tony McDade
Dominique "Rem'mie" Fells
Riah Milton
Jayne Thompson
Selena Reyes-Hernandez
Brian "Egypt' Powers
Brayla Stone
Merci Mack
Shaki Peters
Bree Black
Summer Taylor
Marilyn Cazares
Dior H Ova
Queasha D Hardy
Aja Raquell Rhone-Spears
Kee Sam
Aerrion Burnett
Mia Green
Valera
Michelle Michellyn Ramos Vargas
Felycya Harris
Brooklyn Deshuna
Patsy Andrea Delgado
Ajita Bhuje
Sara Blackwood
Angel Unique

240V
their bo-dies-are-real.
they were
a-
live and now they-re not.
I don-t know
how else to ex plain this to
you. ye a h,
dad says. the gen-
era tor's a go-
od id-
ea.
that could work.

[an apocryphal gospel]

[*I love you, good-night*]

In the darkening pink-gray light,
the grazing deer is quieter than
the chickens who are quieter than
the hungry cat, but only just. I am
anxious about a problem I cannot
recall, or perhaps it's dysphoria, sitting
middle distance between my
shoulder blades and sternum.
I wait for the fireflies. Any minute

they will begin their gentle drifting
upwards. I used to visit my Grandpa
in Appalachia all summer when I was
small and marvel
at their bodies, this little light of mine—
must've presumed they were stepping heavenward.
God would've lost me much
sooner were it not for fireflies.

Oh, here they are now—
the deer grazed on and
the chickens settled in their nesting boxes, but

the firefly searches for evangelion and never
makes it past the treetops.
I hope they're well.
I hope you're well.
I love you, good-night.

[acknowledgments]

Sincere thanks to the editors and staff of the following publications, wherein versions of these poems have appeared:

Vagabond City Lit and *Rio Grande Review*: "the same god who told me being gay was a sin sold me t on the down-low ten years later"

Birdcoat Quarterly: "three bodies and the memory of a fourth while the earth turns slowly"

Sky Island Journal: "theodicy"

Rio Grande Review and *After the Pause*: "when I discover the word 'all'"

After the Pause: "death of the hen in three syllables"

Anti-Heroin Chic: "hymns: untitled," "monologue regarding appalachia, voiced to an empty room," and "I love you, good-night"

[author bio]

Em J Parsley lives in rural Kentucky and received their MFA in Creative Writing from the University of Texas at El Paso. When he's not receiving divine poetic wisdom, he cobbles together a living through English adjunct teaching jobs. When he's not teaching, he's giving his cats a million kisses on the forehead, and if he still has time after that, he sees some of his work published in journals such as A*NMLY*, *Birdcoat Quarterly*, *Screen Door Review*, and *Every Day Fiction*. Their poetry was a finalist for Frontier Poetry Chapbook Contest, the Robert Phillips Poetry Chapbook Prize, and the Wolfson Press Chapbook Award. This is their first chapbook.